So not the easiest of years.... hopefully others experiences will bring comfort to 2017 love Siobhan & Frank xxxx

Poems

That Come to Mind

For those who love someone

with dementia

Linda E. Austin

Moonbridge Publications

ISBN: 978-0-9772323-2-1

Moonbridge Publications, 701 Simmons Ave,
St. Louis, Missouri 63122, USA

http://moonbridgebooks.com

For my mother

My mother is in the firm grip of Alzheimer's disease. I visit her at the nursing home almost every day, yet she is always surprised to see me. I chat with caregivers and other residents and their families, and help as I can in little ways.

The following poems were inspired by caring for my mother and by my visits to the nursing home. I hope you will find them sweet despite the pain behind them. Perhaps they will give comfort to those searching for words to describe what they are going through in their own journeys with dementia care.

Dementia/Alzheimers has come to heavily haunt the human condition. Both mother and daughter facing this scourge in *Poems That Come to Mind* find that each day is "buried deeper" and is harder to find. Each delicately and fiercely imaged poem is a tribute to perseverance and survival and a lesson for us all.

--Walter Bargen, First Poet Laureate of Missouri

Poems

That Come to Mind

I reach my hand
into the day
searching its pockets
for a penny
to buy a new beginning

I went to see the cherry blossoms today

but their season was over

instead I reveled

in the blooms of crabapples

in the deep, dark well
when the light at the top fades
it is only you
and the god you believe in
and sometimes that's not enough

we argue again
over nothing important
neither understands
we talk of different pieces
of the same scary puzzle

I answer the phone
tell her it's not a hotel
her pretty new home
there are people there to help
so nice, she'll never be lost

She wants to believe
but it doesn't seem quite right
come and get me now
yes it's so beautiful here
but I'm ready to go home

Mozart

a song with no words
a familiar refrain plays
over and over
an old man closes his eyes
sings his memories of Air

Let's break out of here,
she whispered to a friend.
But we'll get lost!
No we won't, I know the way,
sure of a homing instinct
that will lead her
to the house across town
where her life lies waiting.

Some days I am known
right away her face brightens
for a long lost friend
How did you know I was here?
I can only smile

She's distant today
mind half closed until I leave
and then, "Drive safely!"
She smiles as I stare at her
surprised by sudden headlights

an old song
pulls a string of memory
unraveling time

they gather outside
old love songs play in the sun
present melts to past
don't make good songs anymore
but soft breezes still kiss cheeks

pink magnolias
we both nap in the spring breeze
no thoughts needed

spring comes 'round again
pale memories blossoming
some lost forever
caught in the space of clouds
that will never float away

cherry blossoms gone
but their story lingers on
I turn the pages

we sit side by side
holding hands in the soft sun
soon we fade away
dozing in warm nothingness
lost in the dove's lamenting

it's only a game
the two of them played
entwining smiles

we sit together
holding hands in silence
no room for words
it's just the two of us
with nothing else between

the stories still there
buried deeper as each day
turns to shadows
living in a dappled realm
the past shivers in the sun

On Mother's Day
all the daughters come to visit
looking just like their mothers
before they imagined that
instead of feeding their children
they would be fed
and roses would never
look so beautiful

She eyes the newcomer,
a tall and handsome man,
maybe a silver-haired lover
floating in her past.
She asks, Do you mind
if I call you sweetheart?
But like the past
he is out of reach.

I lift up the spoon
filled with pasta in cream sauce
wake up and eat now
the spoon touches her lips
her eyes open and she smiles

My mother watches
wondering what I'm doing
helping another
this friend she doesn't know
who sits with her at each meal

I leave deflated
my heart pricked by despair
some days are like that
only mist and sleep gather
the air we breathe so heavy

Mary, Mary, he called.

I'm not her, I say.

But you look just like her!

Later, Mary arrives.

I go to see my twin

who is very tall

with short blonde hair

while I am short

with long dark hair

A red leaf falls
from an old magazine
a dried reminder
of when she wrote letters
sent with pieces of the past

Landscapes

She
who once painted birch trees
reflected in a still pond
and dark pines
moody in the snow
can no longer paint
even a single tulip.
She holds the brush
in a frail hand
unsteady and uncertain.
Her mind cannot stay in the lines
or connect the dots.
A red smear marks the trail
of her disease.
She falls asleep
and I wonder if her dream
will be of beautiful trees
or whether her thoughts
can only be
still water.

I see the pages
of history in his eyes
an old Marine
he wears his cap with pride
fighting a new kind of war

Who are you, she asks
studying my face
but then she smiles
as memory finds her
and spares me for another day

He smiles at me
when I ask him questions
he can't answer.
When I smile back
and pat his arm
he reaches for my hand
and won't
let
go.

Leaving

I have to go now.
Where are you going?
Home to fix dinner.
I'll come with you.

How do you say no
to someone who needs you
more than anything else
in the world?
Your only chance at sanity
is to know that after you've left
it will be as though
you had never been there
except for the slight warmth
left over from your kiss.

I sing to you
songs you taught me when I was small
songs from when you were small
not knowing the words would someday hold
more meaning than we could ever imagine

Crescent moon so high
I hear my mother singing
an old lullaby

The moon this night
so full yet not a drop spills
the night so bright
we make our wishes
poured into the Milky Way

Rain wet streets
the windshield blurs with tears
the wipers can't reach

For Katie

In her last days
life seems exquisitely sweet
She dreams of lilies
that bloom in the garden
the one that awaits her

The rustle of wings
in the corner, love waiting
whispering, come home

an old sketch by my mother

About the poems:

My mother is Japanese and I am half. I have embraced my Asian heritage and love many things Japanese, especially art and poetry where a richness of experience is conveyed using a sparse style.

Many of the poems in this book are in the style of haiku and tanka. Tanka begin as haiku, but have two more lines.

Other books:

My mother's stories of life growing up in Japan around the time of WWII were published as Cherry Blossoms in Twilight: Memories of a Japanese Girl, 2007, by Moonbridge Publications

The gradual loss of memories, of the ability to complete a thought, of the mind to connect with the body, are the frightening and tragic symptoms of those suffering Alzheimer's or other dementia-inducing disorders. Our beloveds are just as dismayed and confused by what they see happening to themselves as are their family and friends.

Please contact the Alzheimer's Association in your area or online to find help and support. Their classes are an invaluable resource for understanding and learning how to handle the symptoms of these heartbreaking disorders.

http://www.alz.org/
24-hour Helpline: 1.800.272.3900

Other recommended resources:

Learning to Speak Alzheimer's : A Groundbreaking Approach for Everyone Dealing with the Disease by Joanne Koenig Coste

Creating Moments of Joy by Jolene Brackey

19436380R00028

Printed in Great Britain
by Amazon